I0486594

$uccess Without College - Roadmap to Plumber

By Christine Axsmith

Special thanks to my husband Justin, who is always a great support and source of fun.

Copyright 2018 Christine Axsmith
Published by Success Without College Publications

Table of Contents

You Can Do It, Too

Three little boys were always late for school. They would wait for the train to come by and run through the smoke it left and then go to school.

One of those boys went to prison for life; the other went to a hospital for the criminally insane, and the third little boy was my Father.

My uncle, a former President of the AFL-CIO for Pennsylvania, called my father the "most successful person he had ever known." I agree.

In Roadmap to Plumber, I am telling you what my Father and others taught me about real success, American-style.

Life is choices. Every day of your life you make a hundred little decisions that either point you towards your goals or not. You can choose to sleep in all day, or not. Or you can decide to take half an hour a day to learn a new language or to play the guitar. It's up to you.

This book is for the people who are willing to choose work and courage over hiding behind conventional wisdom. If you are willing to work as hard as someone who goes to college, then you can be a plumber. My Father could only afford two years of college because I was born. But he worked for hours on weekends, evenings, and holidays to prepare for his professional engineering license test, even though most people who take that test already have a four-year degree.

He failed the test the first time, but kept working at it until he succeeded. My Father is an amazing man in many respects.

My most indelible memories growing up were sitting with my Father and my sisters at the dining room table, all of us doing math and studying for a test. Give the children in your family the gift my Father gave me; a family memory of studying and working together. Your decision to take this path will affect everyone around you, as well as yourself. Do it! You have only the future in front of you.

Not everyone has the option of college. This is not an anti-college book. It is a book for any age for people who want to work hard. You just have to want it. Choose your future, don't let it just happen to you.

The Big Lie

You don't need college to be an American success story. The idea that college is a necessity is new. It never used to be that way.

Since 2008, the United States has lost millions of jobs. Many of those jobs are not coming back. Right now, many attorneys are being replaced by software programs, where someone can file a lawsuit just by answering a few questions on a website. No one thought that would start happening when factories were sent overseas. They thought it would happen to somebody else.

But there are jobs that cannot be sent overseas, or replaced by a robot. These are the types of jobs my books will describe to you.

I want to help you. My superpower is learning a new career from scratch. I started my professional life writing information systems security policies, have tested large information systems, started a dog walking business, became a court-appointed attorney for the elderly and mentally disabled, started a sole practitioner law firm focused on real estate litigation, and now am a writer.

We are all told that the unemployment rate is very low, but that isn't true. It is actually around 10%. The low unemployment numbers reported on the news are based on phoning 3,500 people during a weekday and asking if they have a job. There is no fact-checking at all. Nobody looks to see if they are telling the truth. Actually, the last thing they want in those numbers is the truth. If people knew the extent of America's unemployment, they would be even angrier than they were during the last election.

There is another number economists use to determine the unemployment rate: U6 unemployment rate. That number is calculated by counting the number of people who were getting a W-2 paycheck and subtracting the number of people who were on W-2 jobs and then later received unemployment benefits and who did not get another job. As of the writing of this book, the unemployment rate, the real one, is 9.4%.

Of course, if you are being told that the unemployment rate is historically low and you don't have a job, it implies that you are at fault. Also not true.

It is equally untrue that you need a college degree to be a success in America. You are being told, and even sold, the idea that college debt is a smart move to get a degree. The underlying promise in this sales pitch is that, with a degree, you will be able to get a well-paying job.

I graduated law school with so much debt; it defined my choices for the next 15 years. I couldn't take jobs I wanted, or own a car because of my student loan debt. If there is some way to help young people avoid this circumstance I want to do it. So I wrote this book.

Nowhere in the famous Horatio Alger stories based on The American Dream does anybody go to college. Many successful Americans did not go to college at first. That can be you. This book is for people who want to become a plumbing professional. Other books in this series $uccess Without College Roadmap will be written for other types of work. Each book will be a standalone roadmap to a profession, not just a job.

A profession means you have valuable skills that you can take with you for the rest of your career. A career is how you build those skills from one job to another. A successful career is when people in your industry know your name, know some of your work history, and can take a good guess at your skill set - just by hearing your name. A profession is the most important investment you will make in your lifetime. Your skills are something that can never be taken from you. If your profession is going to be plumbing, then you need to invest time and effort to get there.

Nothing in life is about passing a test and getting what you want. A certificate does not make you a businessperson, and it won't get you a job. That's why getting a college degree is not a recipe for success.

This book explains the real, old-fashioned American Dream. It is different from the you-must-go-to-college-or-your-life-is-over message. Success is not what you thought it was. Neither is what success looks like, let alone how to get there. This book tells you how to see success, and how to go and get it.

Your Advantage in Not Having a Degree

No Student Loans

These days, many college graduates have huge debts and no serious prospect of work. The "deal" had been broken where a job could be expected if you graduated from college. Now high school students are encouraged to take out student loans, and no one pretends that they should expect a job upon graduation from college.

You can take control of your life, and your career, by systematically following this Roadmap to Plumber book, and then going and getting it. It takes social courage to be good at something. You put doing a task first. You work hard, even with doubts. You don't let what other people say or do take you off the track to your goal. That is success.

Why Should You Be Hired Over a College Graduate?

- You work harder.
- You are mature and have had jobs with responsibility in the past, and your resume reflects this.
- Good school attendance record.
- You will show up on time and get the task completed.
- You don't need to be told how important you are, or what a good job you are doing more than once in six months.

- You know that your opinion doesn't mean much, and what you can do means much more.

Roadmap to Plumber provides the step-by-step plan to becoming a career and a living that will not be replaced by computers.

And you won't need a degree.

Who This Book is For

Roadmap to Plumber is written for anyone who wants have a starting point and a roadmap to becoming a plumber or a job in the plumbing profession without getting a degree. This book is to enable anyone who can do the work to become successful.

Roadmap to Plumber is designed to help someone become a plumber, no matter the level of experience. It provides a roadmap to follow in an overwhelming sea of information on this topic. It provides many links to free education.

What This Book Will Do

Roadmap to Plumber gives you everything you need to get started on a plumbing career without college.

You need a good starting point for your own self-education. Roadmap to Plumber will tell you about teaching yourself skills, and how to get a job from there.

"College" is a word that is shorthand for a lot of things other than education. When employers ask for a "college degree," they really want some professionalism, middle-class appearance and manners, maturity, and moderate intelligence, and discipline. You don't need to get into $100,000 of debt to offer this to an employer.

Roadmap to Plumber will tell you what those middle-aged hiring managers are secretly thinking - and worrying about - when they interview you. I know, because I was one of them.

What This Book Won't Do

Roadmap to Plumber will empower you, but there are things it cannot do for you.

If you are going to buck the trend of the people and community around you, you need to be prepared for certain things. You are going to start to feel disconnected from that community. You are going to feel scared. Norman Podhoretz wrote an excellent book "Making It" about what it feels like to rise to the middle class. It is an old book, and probably won't be in your local library. He describes his feelings of awkwardness around the new people he met. He shows his shame at not understanding what they are talking about. And this was one brilliant guy. Yes, his story does include going to college, but his emotional journey is one that you may have to make as well.

When I started school in Philadelphia, it was a dramatic change from the small town I had known all my life. Market Street divided the campus and was a major, busy street. The problem was, I had no experience crossing a busy four lane street in a major city and would often get stuck in the middle, on the double lines, when the light changed, while traffic buzzed right by me. I was too scared to move. People had to run out to the middle of Market Street, people I didn't even know, and walk me to the curb.

This happened repeatedly. Other students knew me as the girl who would get stuck in the middle of the street for years. It was very humiliating, plus I was the only one this happened to. Seriously. I can look back on that feeling of shame and say, "So what?" That's right. Who cares? Would I trade a lifetime of opportunity and growth to avoid feeling that again? No. Don't you, either. What embarrasses you right now will make a great story at a party in later years. Trust me. What makes an interesting dinner guest is someone who laughs at their mistakes, not someone who tells everyone about their accomplishments. Let other people do that for you.

Many people cannot do it. They are not strong enough. They are too afraid of what family or friends will think. Now, most likely, family and friends will be very proud of you. But the fear that there will be a separation is enough for most young people to quit their dreams. That's a choice affecting the rest of your life.

Wake up and see what is going on out there. This is difficult because you are being told that you need to go to college; college is the only way to be an American success, and only losers don't go to college. The news supports this view and TV shows endorse this view. It is the lie that you will make enough money if you just get that college degree.

Not true.

The American Dream vs. The American Day Dream

The American Dream Defined:

"That dream of a land in which life should be better and richer and fuller for everyone, with opportunity for each according to ability or achievement."
- James Treslow Adams.

Notice it doesn't say anything about college or student loans.

What you have been told is a lie. You can spend a lot of money and time investing in this lie, or you can choose something different for yourself.

Owning a small business that is successful, where the owner can earn the respect of his peers and community, and gather a small bit of wealth about themselves and their family is the American Dream. It is where hard work and honesty lead to material comfort and respect. There is no need to lie and steal to survive, which is the reality in other places.

A "dream" does not mean something is not true; it just means that it is a story we tell ourselves about ourselves. It reveals the core values of a society and a country. The "American Dream" is one of the most powerful on Earth.

The American Dream is that anyone can rise above his or her circumstances to achieve success in the United States. If you are willing to work hard, be honest, take risks and not get into debt, the American Dream promises you success in America.

The American Day Dream is what advertising sells you. It is the lives shown in movies where a waitress can afford to live in a large apartment in Manhattan, or where an Assistant District Attorney drives a Mercedes. It is where everyone has a large, flat screen TV.

The American Dream is not getting into debt.

The American Day Dream causes you to look at your neighbors to judge yourself. It creates fears of teeth that aren't white enough, a recent advertising invention. It makes you worry that you secretly reek of body odor and no one wants to tell you, but they all gag behind you in the elevator at work.

The American Dream means you take care of the basics, and don't listen to commercials about what is important.

The American Day Dream tells you that all that matters is getting into a good college. It tells you that your life will be made or broken based on the college you attend. It tells you that any amount of debt is worth it for this class membership. They are wrong. The American Day Dream tells you to get into horrible debt, and it's OK because you will get a fantastic job and be able to pay it all back. Not true.

The American Dream tells of a young person who works hard and is honest and can support themselves and their family.

You need to start identifying the American Day Dream and its influence all around you.

Debt has always been a very un-American thing. It's only for the last sixty or so years that debt has been sold as OK - and it took a lot of advertising to get there.

Americans have needed debt to maintain their standard of living for a while. Americans were, for most of this country's existence, repelled by debt. There was a very strong prejudice against it.

We need to get back to the American Dream in this country. And nothing is more fundamentally American than starting your own career.

Where To Start

"If I had to do it over again, I'd become a plumber." Albert Einstein

"The plumber protects the health of the nation."

The Last of the Superheroes

The $uccess Without College Roadmap series of books focuses on jobs that will be there for the next forty years, and nothing fits the bill for that better than plumber. Plumbers need to be creative problem-solvers, good at dealing with people in distress, and willing to learn as they continue in their career. But no matter what job you get, you will need to get more training. All the jobs that do not require continual training will be replaced by computers or robots.

A plumber is what I call a Superhero profession. You help people in need, solve their problem, and then go to the next emergency across town. You leave behind happy and relieved people who stand in their driveway, waving goodbye to you, asking themselves "who was that uniformed person?" Then they open the bill and find out. But the glory lasts a few minutes at least.

But seriously, without proper plumbing, people die of cholera and other diseases. This profession allows civilization to exist.

If you like driving around, meeting new people, and having every day be different, then consider working as a plumber. You get the satisfaction of solving a problem for someone who is really appreciative that you could help them. Then it is back in the truck, off to a new problem. Kind of like a superhero.

An online search for "How to Become a Plumber" does not tell you the steps you have to take, who to talk to, and how to get plumbing courses for free. That is why I wrote this book.

No one is in the schools telling people about these opportunities. High school guidance counselors are not telling students about job possibilities in the trades, and that includes plumbing. Besides, becoming a licensed plumber can lead to many types of jobs, such as a plumbing inspector or plumbing design for construction projects. The earning potential is the sky if you are willing to learn and work hard.

If you don't believe me, how about the billionaire who was the Mayor of New York City? "Young people today should consider a job in plumbing," said Mayor Bloomberg in the New York Daily News.

It is a career for intelligent people for several reasons: you are getting a skill that will always be needed and will only work in a coffee shop for your own amusement, your education is free, you have a job while getting that education, and there are no student loan payments.

"They don't call it college, but it is a five year program. You get paid while you study, the schooling is free and you have a job at the end of it." said Rick, plumber in Maryland.

More than that, the green revolution is not going to happen without plumbers. Frankly, society itself will collapse without plumbers. Plumbers groups have been instrumental in water conservation efforts. Saving $46.3 billion in water and energy with the Water Sense program. "The fact that water and wastewater costs are increasing much faster than energy costs will have a major impact on future decisions concerning all types of equipment and appliances that use both water and energy," H.W. "Bill" Hoffman, P.E. wrote in Contractor magazine.

Plumbers will be installing tankless and solar-powered water heaters because this is what customers will want in the future. Another plumbing innovation is using the heat of the Earth to heat or cool your home, called geothermal HVAC units.

The importance of skilled plumbers can best be seen by the fatal cholera epidemic that killed hundreds of people in Haiti. Cholera is the disease that comes from water contaminated with poop. All of those deaths were the result of bad plumbing. Now imagine the world without people able to prevent it. That's right, you'd be dead.

Any high school kid can get a job in plumbing, provided they can present themselves as mature, hard-working and willing to learn.

Becoming a licensed plumber should be thought of as similar to getting a masters degree. It takes that long and is that much work. The big difference is plumbers don't have student loan debt and cannot be replaced by computers.

Can you work hard, show up, and do what is asked? The job satisfaction is you can visualize the solution and then make it happen. And did I mention, no student loans?

The Payoff

Money

A plumber can make $60-70,000 a year without student loans by the age of 26. It really is the equivalent of having a Masters degree - without the debt and a including a good job.

> The trade off for that is that you can easily make over $100,000. I had one plumber last year who actually net $120,000. He did not really achieve balance — he was away from home a lot and doing one weekend call a month. But he had great compensation and great benefits.
> I can look at my men and I can tell them with all honesty, "In the next ten years, every one of you can

make a million dollars. I can not only provide you a secure working base, but provide security for your retirement too." And not all working trades are doing that. I think that's pretty darn rare. <u>Bob,</u> a plumbing trainer.

Plumbers Will NOT Be Replaced By a Robot

One of the greatest things about becoming a plumber is that you will not be replaced by a robot or a computer. Trust me, I know. Lawyers are being replaced by computer programs. Sites like LegalZoom and others are providing adequate services for the general public. These are not a good option for complicated matters, but people just need basic documents most of the time. But even worse for lawyers are the websites that let people just fill in blanks to create their own lawsuits.

Lawyers used to perform those functions for people. The only thing left is fighting in court which, while fun, has become a game of scrapping over clients. There is less work for a growing number of attorneys. Law schools became a big money-maker for universities, so the supply of law graduates climbed. That, and popular culture, led to an increasing number of law school applicants. By charging expensive tuition to prospective layers, universities banked a lot of money. That there were too many lawyers for the marketplace did not enter the equation.

For a plumber, there are so many types of jobs that can be done. Plumbing skills are just a start. Combined with computer-aided design skills, you could work with construction companies to design plumbing installation, work as a plumbing inspector, or other careers. Starting with plumbing certifications, you can added more training and be eligible for dozens of other jobs.

Earn while you learn

A lot of plumbers have a college degree. It is easy to do because most of plumber training gives college credits. Only five more general college classes are needed to get an Associates degree. So you will get most of a degree for free, while being paid as well.

You will get the last laugh. A lot of careers people are preparing for with college are being replaced by computers. So all the follow-the-rules types who did everything they were told, who got into debt with promises of riches as successful lawyers, are screwed.

What Plumbers Do

Rick was a DJ for ten years before starting to work as plumber. "It felt like I worked in a box." Then he told his uncle, who had a plumbing firm, that he had a few spare days and did he want some help? At the end of two days, he decided plumbing is what he wanted to do.

"It's the freedom. It's amazing." said RIck. "Every day is different. I go from job to job, talk to people, solve their problems."

There are all kinds of plumbing work available to choose from. You can work in new construction for residential or office buildings, or repair in older ones. You can use your plumbing experience, add computer design skills, and design plumbing systems for large new construction. The goal for that job is to make sure that the plumbing systems doesn't run into the electrical and other systems. Then there's Plumbing Inspector, who makes sure builders aren't cutting corners which would result in a massive health crisis.

A more hands-on, practical explanation can be found on this union website.

> United Association - Union of Plumbers, Fitters, Welders, & Service Techs has this definition on their website Ua.org "Our contractors and members are actively engaged in plumbing installation, repair, service and maintenance of piping and plumbing systems and equipment used for drinking (potable)

water distribution, sanitary waste drainage, storm
water systems and gas distribution."
"The Piping Profession"

"We are the unsung heroes. No one thinks of us until they
need us. Where's the prayer for plumbers? Oh, that's
fifteen minutes before they get there." said Rick, a master
plumber from Maryland.

What It Takes To Be a Plumber

A plumber has a combination of skills they use every day. It is why the job is so interesting. And the learning doesn't stop. A plumber works on a team to solve problems, so being a team player is critical.

Mechanical skills

If you can learn how to fix things, have the dexterity to use hand tools, these are the mechanical skills used as a plumber. Years ago, high schools sorted people according to whether the school thought they were mechanically inclined or not. In practice, they picked a career path for a teenager based on what they had seen of them so far. Some were routed to the trades, like plumber and electrician, and other were put on the college track. About seven years ago, the policy became routing all teens to the college track. Guidance counselors didn't get accolades for anything but the number of students going to college. Trade education was ignored. Now, there's a serious shortage of plumbers and it will only get worse.

> "When I was 15, the school guidance counselor wanted to know if I was on the academic track or the trade track. How am I going to know that at 15? But that's what they want you to decide. Fortunately, I chose trade." Jason, a master plumber.

An apprentice plumber will need to lift things, install pipe in the air and ground, solder and braise. Braising is above 840 degrees, soldering is below that temperature. Braising is important for medical gas, glue, making hangers to hold pipes in air, thrust blocks to make sure pipe holds together underground. Whenever you see a water main break, often it is when thrust block moves around the pipe.

Communications skills

Plumbers are called when something goes seriously wrong. It follows that people are upset when you arrive. You really must be able to talk to people who want their problem solved desperately, but don't really want to pay you all that much.

For example, one thing plumbers hear a lot is "I can get that for $79 at [big box store]." Part of your job is explaining why they need a better quality part or why that cheaper option will not solve their problem.

Another one is installing copper pipes. While copper is expensive, copper pipes are also antimicrobial, whereas plastic is not. If you leave your house for two weeks, algae will grow in plastic pipes that feed into your house.

Plumbing can also involve sensitive matters that must be handled with diplomacy.

Page 27

"When I was a journeyperson, I was asked to clear a trap at a shop steward's house. It was clogged with condoms. When I told him he said, 'I don't use condoms.'" Oops. Technical skills are not the only requirement for a good plumber. Social skills are, too.

Business sense

All plumbers must develop business sense. An apprentice plumber becomes a journeyperson after passing state certifications. Journeyperson plumbers must be able to cost jobs accurately to give estimates to customers. So part of an apprenticeship is learning this universal business skill. That is why you work is important. Don't go to a "churn and burn" plumbing contractor. You won't learn how to deal with customers, and that is a key part of being successful in any business.

Other universal business skills are keeping records of what was done, when it was done, how much it cost you to do, how much of that was labor and how much were materials, what you charged the customer, your profit per job and per day, and what types of tasks have the highest profit margins.

The most important business skill is answering the phone when it rings and returning phone calls right away. It is easy and simple, yet many people do not do it.

Plumbers must have this knowledge in additions to the raw skills. Plumbing is a business.

Soft Skills

We touched on this subject earlier, but here are some specifics.

When you walk into a plumbing business looking for a job, they are assessing you for whether or not you would be a good employee in areas other than intelligence and skills.

A plumbing business is looking for a helpful attitude and a willingness to learn. They want someone who listens to instructions, who won't scare nervous housewives with sagging pants and a lot of tattoos. You can show your butt off on your own time.

The entire career of a plumber is spent working with others. You learn on a team and you work on a team. You need to get along on a team.

Plumbing is very profitable, but is hard work. Your work history should indicate that you are not afraid of hard work, or showing up on time.

Cleanish record

Since a plumber drives in the company truck, for insurance reasons, there needs to be a clean driving record. That means no speeding tickets or serious car accidents. There is some flexibility here because we were all young and just learning to drive at some point, but no drunk driving arrests.

Another insurance-related point is no "visible" arrest record. If you were young at the time of the arrest, it can be expunged, and won't interfere with getting a clearance. Recruiters for the plumbing profession understand that often the difference between an arrest record and a clean record is that someone's parents could afford expensive attorneys. Plumbers work in nuclear reactors and other places that require a clearance so this is important.

Brains

We are not talking about differential equations, or other abstract math. A plumber has to calculate with fractions and decimals, quickly and in their head. They use geometry and trigonometry to figure the angles to get the pieces of pipe that is needed, so you will need to understand the math also. I'm sure you know this, but brains does not mean high grades necessarily.

"When you get good at it, you get really fast," explained Tim, a plumber from New Jersey. "Experienced plumbers have cheat methods to avoid the math, because less math is less mistakes. But to understand them, you really have to see them. That's why having a teacher with lots of field experience in plumbing is so important."

Plumbers read and interpret building blueprints regularly, and need to understand the implications of what they see.

"A lot of times the problem people call you for is only a symptom of the real problem. A plumber has to be able to find the root cause of what is going on." said Tom, an experienced plumber.

Computer skills are essential as much of the mechanical parts are computerized in newer systems. Manufacturers hold classes for their equipment, which can be attended for free, but you will need a foundational understanding of computers to understand the topic.

Older buildings require hands-on training, and any aspiring plumber will also have to be able to learn that way as well. "Plumbing is affected by what is going on in the world at that time. So if we are in a war, it will affect the plumbing fixtures and how they are made. If a new plastic is being used, the parts installed during those years will be made of the new material. The materials change as the economy changes.

The practical result is many houses have a patchwork of different pipes and devices, with different sizes, because people want a band-aid fix most of the time. A plumber has to measure everything and adapt new materials to old materials. There is no book for that. You will need to know where to get the parts in your area because the big box stores won't have it.

Brawn

Physical fitness is a requirement. Luckily, you are young and can get into shape easily. Try it at 53. No picnic.

Plumbers work long hours and need physical stamina. They need the strength to lift pipes and toilets and kitchen sinks. You have to be able to climb on roofs and be outside in all weather. Good news: human beings are waterproof.

Related Jobs

The third most powerful person in NJ is a master plumber

Plumbing is so essential to civilization and the survival of the human species that training in that field can be used in many other fields, and in fact is a requirement to working in the occupations below:

- Medical plumbing - involves delivery of pure oxygen, CO_2, nitrogen in medical offices and hospitals. "Medical gas in hospitals"
- Plumbing design - use of CAD systems to design plumbing in large construction projects.
- Commercial plumber - specialization, such as medical plumbing license, working well with other tradesmen on site and learning from them, reading blueprints and analysing the plumbing design for a large building, or a commercial plumber can work on restaurant and gas station plumbing.
- Residential plumber
- Hydronic in-floor heating
- Solar thermal panels
- Heat pumps
- Cross-connection control
- Fire protection
- Sprinker
- HVAC
- Data centers

- CAD design- draw buildings
- Pipefitter

Roadmap

The career path to becoming a plumber starts with becoming a plumbers assistant or going to school and then becoming an apprentice. Either way, after taking state certifications, you become a journeyperson. After about four years of learning, both in the classroom and outside of it, a journeyperson takes the Master Plumber exam. From start to finish, it takes about six years.

There are two ways to get started on this career path: school and apprenticeship.

School

A high school diploma is a must. You can attend classes at a community college and then get a job as an apprentice plumber. After a certain number of work hours, determined by the state you are working in, you can take the Journeyperson certification tests.

College credits are built into the United Association plumber training program, for example. You can earn college credits, for free, while learning how to make a lot of money. Other opportunities for training at Associated Plumbing, Cooling, Heating Contractors. Online classes are offered there to prepare you for an apprenticeship in plumbing, and more are available as you advance. While not free, the classes are reasonably priced.

Apprenticeship

An apprenticeship has lots of on the job training, and you are paid while you learn. The question to ask before working with a plumbing company is whether or not they offer Journeyperson or Master plumbing training for free to apprentices. Most apprentices are in their early to mid-twenties.

An employer must be registered with the U.S. Department of Labor if they are offering an apprenticeship. These are called "registered apprenticeship programs" and must have a written Apprenticeship Agreement If it isn't a registered apprentice program, it is a scam. If there is no written Apprenticeship Agreement, it is a scam.

An apprenticeship is a four year commitment and the classes are free, but you don't get paid to take the classes, only the day job. Classes are often two nights a week for three hours a night, for four years. After that, an apprentice must pass state board certification tests.

To find a reputable plumber, read google reviews, ask local apartment buildings who they use, and contact the Better Business Bureau and do a Google Scholar search to see if they have been in any lawsuits.

Union and non-union

Unions spend millions on training, and send highly trained people. You will need to apply, pass a test, interview, and pass a drug test. Any union program has their contractors registered and are in total compliance.

Google the local union, find out when they are taking apprentices.

Trade associations offer training programs as well, as mentioned above.

School Is Not Over Kids

The National Apprenticeship and Training Standards require that minimum of 144 hours per year of apprenticeship training be provided to each trainee. Related training is a requirement. You will need some knowledge in math, science, safety laws, basic measurement and reading a blueprint. An apprenticeship means learning on the job by observation, in a classroom and by practice.

You can get related training at a vocational program at high school, a community college course or a training program at the plumber business where you work.

———

Questions to Ask

Does the program prepare you for the state certification exams?
Do you have a registered apprenticeship program?
Do you have a written Apprenticeship Agreement?
Have all the teachers worked in the field as plumbers for over 15 years?
Are all the teachers master plumbers?
If the answer to any of these questions is "no," then don't take that program.

Pitfalls

There is no state-to-state reciprocity in the trades, so you need to get licensed again for another state.

Be sure to get a job where you interact with people as well as learn technical skills. Communication is a critical part of being a successful plumber

Schools are realizing they need to create trade programs again, but are not hiring plumbers to teach. Years of hand-on experience cannot be replaced by a cross-trained math teacher. Ask the hard questions to protect your future self.

Get a Job

The Person Who Hires You

All people have stupid stories they tell themselves, and people who make hiring decisions are the same. They say to themselves, "Well this guy hasn't worked in two years, so he'll have a hard time getting up in the morning because what he's been doing is lying on his couch for the last two years."

Of course, you know that you have been selling your living room furniture, learning how to score day-old food from grocery stores, shopping at goodwill, and hand knitting presents for your niece and nephew from old unraveled sweaters. You know that it takes a lot of work to eat and keep the lights on when you're broke.

The same is true about a college degree. People will tell themselves: well, my cousin's daughter had to go to college for this, so the guy in front of me needs to do that, too.

We aren't out to change people's thinking. We are going to work with it to get what we want.

Put Yourself in Their Shoes

If you were a middle-aged manager interviewing a young person, what would you want in an employee? Would you want someone who appears to drink a lot and sometimes doesn't remember everything that happened during that time? BTW- if you don't remember what happens when you drink sometimes, you need my other book: Alcoholic or Problem Drinker?

You have to put yourself in the manager's chair when trying to get them to hire you. All day long, middle managers deal with two groups of people: upper management and employees.

Employees get assigned work, and they do it with varying degrees of success. Some employees need to be reminded all the time to get their task done. Some employees will get the task done very quickly but always with sloppy mistakes. Some employees will ignore what you ask them to do and hand in what they think should be done.

And this is only one part of dealing with employees. The other is babysitting. What would your day be like if you had to spend an hour talking to a 45-year-old man about why it really shouldn't matter that his desk is two inches smaller than someone else's? Or if a group of employees decides they don't like someone else in the office and come to you one by one to complain about that person, after having coordinated their stories? Or two people who have a multi-day fight over where the printer is placed? These are only three examples of the kind of petty nonsense that middle managers have to deal with. Don't be one of those people.

Upper management gives deadlines to middle managers that are based on selling products, not on how long it takes to do the work. Basically, the sometimes-crazy thing you are asked to do may not be coming from your boss. So have sympathy for the person.

Resume

Your spelling and grammar must be perfect. Yes, English class mattered. It is the one subject that signals you have a good education. When people see your resume and cover letter, they are looking for grammar and spelling errors. If they don't see any, you are given credit for having intelligence. You may be seeking a job as an engineer and believe that it doesn't matter how good your spelling is. You would be wrong. Bad spelling shows sloppiness, and bad grammar shows ignorance. No one wants to hire that.

Your resume doesn't say who you are. It says, "I can get this job done for you!" It says, "Hire me!" It says, "I am not a problem!" and "I can do the boring parts of computer programming without complaining."

No one is hiring the real you. They are renting what you can do for them. Employers put out a call for people based on what they think they need. Your resume needs to reflect what they think they want, right back at them. See below, The Robot That Hires You.

Don't choose unusual paper or formatting. It says to a prospective employer that you can't work within a system and that you want to be the center of attention. This may be good for an artistic or creative job, as an interior designer, for instance. But not for a plumber.

Create a LinkedIn profile. LinkedIn is also your resume. Fill it in and add information on your experience. A college degree or the GPA are only there to show you are not stupid. There are other less expensive ways to do that.

Your resume should show what specific tasks you can complete, not just the name of the hardware or brand of the equipment.

Walking Through the Door

"Skills can be taught, professionalism cannot." - Reddit

What Nobody Wants

- Someone who can't get along with other people.
- Someone who steals.
- Someone who might come into the workplace one day and start shooting people.
- Someone with a drug or alcohol problem.

It used to be that you just had to keep controversial stuff off your resume. Now a potential employer can read all about you on social media. Be low risk. You may be young enough to think that showing people that you got drunk is funny, but nobody wants to hire that. So don't post a photo or video of yourself drunk, getting drunk, or committing a crime on the Internet. Anywhere. People want an employee that is no trouble, so look like you are no trouble from their perspective.

Understanding Social Media

Use social media to your advantage by adding connections to professional associations related to your goal.

Avoid any speech that implies you may not be able to work with all kinds of people. The thing about working is that you are going to be exposed to people you are not choosing to associate with. You are kind of stuck with them. No manager wants to hire someone who requires special measures because they can't work with, or for a certain group of people.

This is America. There are all kinds of people here. They aren't going anywhere, no matter what you think. They all have some money that your company wants to make theirs. That won't happen if one of their employees is seen as someone who can't get along with albino Pygmies.

Now there may not be a lot of albino Pygmies out there. Your prospective employer may not have great concerns about the albino Pygmy market. But they will be concerned about hiring someone who can't get along with an entire group of people. And not only that, someone who announces it to the world.

So don't do it. The only real race that counts in America is the green dollar.

For example, President Obama smokes cigarettes. So did Jackie Kennedy Onassis. To cultivate a certain image of themselves, neither has had a photo taken of them smoking a cigarette. We all know about these two people, and have opinions about them. But it is in no way based on the visual impression of them smoking, which would alter perceptions of them a great deal.

Now smoking is not illegal. It is not associated with cruelty or animal abuse. But the very picture of someone smoking will alter perceptions about him or her. My point is, you create lasting impressions about yourself by revealing personal information. It could prevent you from getting a job, even if you ace the interview. Don't do that to yourself.

If hiring managers are afraid they might hire an irresponsible person, they will be looking for warning signs in a social media profile of debauchery and useless, hung over employees who call in sick all the time. Of course, they may secretly wish they could do all that, and decide you must be that way, too.

The people hiring you are older. One universal thing about older people: they don't remember all the drugs and drinking they did when they were your age. They also don't remember the laws they broke or all the lies they told to get laid.

That's why you have to clean up your social media profile.

Who They Want to Hire

Potential employers are judging you, and asking themselves the following questions:

- Can you show up on time?
- Can you write an email that others can understand, or is it written in text-speak?
- Are you going to be on your best behavior at a meeting with a client? That means no cursing or slang. Can you sit up straight in a chair, say please and thank you, sit still, and listen unless someone asks you a direct question? You will understand your role is to support the senior person from your team, and you won't complain about the dress code or the food in the cafeteria. As an aside, you will also realize no one cares what you think, but only what you can do for them at work.
- Will you dress and groom yourself like an adult or a child? Specifically, will you need to be told that shorts, flip-flops, belly shirts, spandex, and yoga pants are not appropriate at work?
- Can you park in a parking garage, get parking validated and make it to the correct floor to the correct meeting room on time?
- Can you talk to a senior level employee without slang or cursing?

- Can you admit you don't know something?
- Disciplined enough to come in the earliest?
- Do you want it enough to be the last to leave the office?

7% Will Be Fired in Two Years

You are not finished when you get the job. That point is only the beginning.

Many employers hire new employees with the idea that 7% of them will be fired in two years. It's called "attrition." So as soon as you start your job, you are competing against your co-hires to still be there in 2 years.

Keep that mindset in deciding to get to work early, don't waste time at work, and delivering your work on time.

Getting the Next Job

You will get future jobs by being recommended by your co-workers. Recruiters are very expensive; no one wants to use one. Also, recruiters have the attention spans of crack addicts. They get together on Mondays and compare notes on jobs that need to be filled, and it's as if the previous 52 weeks never happened. Just expect it. And they are very expensive; any company saves a lot of money by getting references from someone they are hiring instead of using headhunters. Keep that in mind regarding how you treat your coworkers.

They will be your source of jobs for the rest of your career.

Conclusion

If you are willing to work hard, study on your own and work on a team to learn new skills, you can be a plumber.

The actions in this book provide a roadmap to becoming a successful plumber without going to college. It is a series of steps that other plumbers I interview took to get there, and you can too.

The most important thing, and the hardest, will be to stick to the roadmap after a few weeks, when the initial excitement wears off.

It is like what an author experiences. Right now, I am sitting here on a beautiful afternoon, typing on my computer with no idea if anyone will read this book. My Mom will buy a copy, but probably won't read it. Many days in the past year have been spent working without any guarantee of result. I just have to do the work anyway.

I may not know if this book will sell more than ten copies, but if I don't write it, I know it won't. So take the risk. There is a need for plumbers, and you can meet that need if you work at it.

Let me know how it works out.

About the Author

Christine Axsmith grew up in a area where most people didn't go to college. Later, her career took a sharp left turn after taking a stand against waterboarding at the CIA. See her entry in Wikipedia.org. From there, she reinvented herself as the owner of a successful dog walking company, a guardian for the elderly and disabled, a trial attorney and a writer. These experiences taught her how to learn from successful people and to draw a roadmap to recreate their success. In recent years, as lawyers started getting replaced by software, it sparked Christine Axsmith's interest in this topic.

Christine Axsmith has been published by NIST and NSA regarding information security law, has presented papers at MIT conferences and the International Bar Association, and actively participated in the United Nations Commission on International Trade Law - Electronic Commerce Working Group. Her research on encryption export became required reading at Harvard Law School.

She uses her extensive research skills to provide a roadmap for non-college success in her books by interviewing self-made millionaires and other people in the many fields.

There are many media reports about success without college statistics, and many of them will tell you that the income a person earns is dramatically increased with a college degree.

That was the old days. More than that, only a little over half of college students get a four-year degree. Now, when calculating whether college is a good "investment," you need to include the cost of student loans.

Other Books by this Author

Please visit your favorite book retailer to discover other books by Christine Axsmith:

$uccess Without College Roadmap Series
Roadmap to Software Developer
Roadmap to Plumber
Frankenstein - The Robot That Hires You

Connect with Christine Axsmith

I really appreciate you reading my book! Here are my social media coordinates:

$uccess Without College - Roadmapto Software Developer
www.successwithoutcollege.net
podcast:Success Without College
Instagram:SuccessWithoutCollege
Twitter:@SuccessWithout2

www.ingramcontent.com/pod-product-compliance
Lightning Source LLC
Chambersburg PA
CBHW021928170526
45157CB00005B/2227